The eMPoWR Source Series

The Foundations of Business Consulting

Tiffany Joy Greene, MBA
&
Joseph Romello

OWL
PUBLISHING

Owl Publishing, LLC.
www.owlpublishinghouse.com

717-925-7511

ISBN: 978-1-949929-87-4

Library of Congress Control Number: In Process

DEDICATION

To our fellow and emerging business consultants who strive to serve as purposeful, productive, and positive change agents for their clients.

CONTENTS

ACKNOWLEDGMENTS

Thank you to our families for being ever-patient while we put the words to paper and for listening to us (or smiling and nodding) while we brainstormed ideas and concepts. Additionally, thank you to Lara Paparo for taking us through our first journey as book authors. This has been an amazing experience, and we look forward to many more adventures.

CHAPTER 1

What Is a Business Consultant, and What Skills Are Needed?

"The difficulty lies, not in the new ideas, but in escaping from the old ones."

– John Maynard Keynes

A business consultant is a person who helps organizations improve their performance and efficiency. In essence, a business consultant helps organizations solve business challenges, thereby serving as constructive change agents.

Often, organizations hire business consultants to gain perspective and an outsider's opinion of their business practices and foundational standing, and because they "can't see the forest for the trees." What does this mean?

Sometimes a person is just too close to the situation to be able to see the big picture. Outside perspective provides clarity. Have you ever played a game of Scrabble or Bananagrams, while finding yourself staring at your letters with sheer frustration and annoyance because "these are the worst letters in the history of the game?" You feel stuck. After such pensive thoughts, someone walks by you, and says, "Wow! Look at that. You have an amazing wordplay right there, and they whisper the word to you." On one hand, you are thrilled because you are no longer stuck, and you have an opportunity to win the game. However, on the other hand, you wonder, "Why didn't I see that?" Sometimes business is like a game of Scrabble or Bananagrams. All you can see are the letters because you have been staring at them too long. It becomes a challenge to see them reorganized in a new way that works.

Business consultants work with their clients to get unstuck and grow. Some of the ways that consultants assist organizations include:

- Identifying problems
- Providing expertise in a specific market
- Initiating change
- Providing objectivity
- Teaching and training employees
- Eliminating staff
- Reviving an organization
- Creating new businesses, products, or services
- Influencing people
- Supplementing existing staff

Business consultants are change agents. Their number

one mission is to identify opportunities for constructive change. To yield positive change, business consultants must:

- **Discover** – To discover, a business consultant must spend time with the organization to observe, ask questions, and learn. The client must provide the requested information to the consultant and not hold back.

- **Evaluate** – After spending time in the discovery phase, a business consultant must evaluate their findings to find opportunities for constructive change.

- **Remain Objective** – Business consultants should not be influenced by "office politics" while evaluating opportunities for constructive change. They should be able to evaluate problems that management and ownership may not see.

- **Identify Opportunities** – Business consultants identify opportunities to grow the business, increase profits, and boost efficiency, otherwise stated as providing opportunities for constructive change.

- **Assist in Implementing Opportunities** – Business consultants work with their clients to implement the opportunities to better the organization. This may include building consensus and commitment among members of the organization, training the client, and improving the organization's effectiveness.

Business consultants are like doctors for organizations. When going to a doctor, patients seek a cure or treatment. However, a good doctor knows what tests and diagnostics to run to properly diagnose a patient. A good doctor looks at the whole body to effectively diagnose and treat the patient. The same is true for a business consultant. Without assessing the whole body or organization, an inaccurate diagnosis will be made, which leads to the wrong, often ineffectual, treatment.

Additionally, just like a doctor, a business consultant should never tell clients what they want to hear. How often have you self-diagnosed yourself using your previous health history, google, and WebMD as your guideposts? How often have your doctors gone along with your self-diagnosis?

Imagine walking into a doctor's office with a sore throat. You've had strep throat so many times in your life, that you are 99.9% certain you have strep throat yet again. You inform your physician that you "know" that you have strep throat, so all she needs to do is give you a prescription for antibiotics. Imagine that she doesn't check your vitals or even look in your throat. She just writes you a prescription, and you are on your way. However, days later, your sore throat has not gone away. You go back to the doctor, and now she runs the diagnostics and looks in your throat. She finds a troubling growth. Had she taken the time to do an independent assessment, you would have received a treatment plan to address the real problem earlier. Just as you do not want to waste time when it comes to your health, you do not want to waste time when it comes to the health of your business.

When most people think of business consultants, their mind goes to major consulting firms, like McKinsey & Company, Boston Consulting Group (BCG), Bain & Company, Accenture Strategy, Deloitte, and others, and these major consulting firms tend to help very large corporations like General Motors, investors like KKR, government entities such as the US Department of Defense, and nonprofits such as the American Red Cross. However, business consultants serve mid-sized businesses, small businesses, microbusinesses, and nonprofit organizations in all industries, as well. Often, the consultants who serve smaller and mid-sized companies are individuals, partners, and small companies.

Types of Business Consultants

There are many types of business consultants, and each type provide a specific service to the organizations they serve. Most business consultants fall within one of the categories below, with some offering more than one special focus areas.

Strategy Consultant

Strategy consultants help organizations identify their long-term goals and vision, and they help organizations make decisions based on long-term goals and data. Additionally, they may help an organization implement the strategies developed.

Management Consultant

Typically, management consultants help organizations create plans to run an organization more effectively and optimally. Many times, they are brought in to help with a specific segment of the organization, like a department, procedure, policy, etc.

Growth Consultant

Growth consultants advise leaders on strategies, policies, and procedures to grow the company. Oftentimes, a growth consultant will have expertise in specific industries.

Financial Advisor Consultant

Financial advisor consultants help leaders determine which business decisions can help or hurt the organization financially and identify risk factors to avoid.

Legal Consultant

Legal consultants advise an organization and its leadership on legal matters to help limit exposure and negative legal repercussions.

Operations Consultant

Operations consultants focus on the implementation of organizational operating procedures. Often, they are tasked with helping with major changes, such as new work practices.

Human Resources (HR) Consultant

HR Consultants work with organizations to identify improved HR practices and policies, and support organizations as they implement new training programs for existing HR teams.

IT Consultant

IT Consultants oversee the implementation of IT infrastructure, and they can help tailor IT infrastructures based on their organizational structure. IT consultants may even provide training to employees on IT systems.

Software Consultant

Software consultants are like IT consultants, but instead of focusing on IT infrastructure, their focus is on software. They are tasked with finding the software that best suits organizational needs.

Marketing Consultant

Marketing consultants work with organizations to help them launch and manage successful marketing campaigns, and they are often tasked with creating marketing plans to generate leads and improve brand awareness.

Sales Consultant

Sales consultants help organizations with creating the most effective sales practices, and they can do this by creating effective sales plans, training, and advising.

Environmental Consultant

Environmental consultants advise organizations on how their activities could negatively impact the environment.

Communications Consultant

Communications consultants share expertise on external and internal communication strategies with organizations.

Fractional business leaders

Business consultants may also serve as fractional leaders or C-Suite members of an organization. Fractional business leaders typically work part-time to help guide an organization. For example, organizations may hire a consultant to serve as a fractional Chief Operations Officer, Chief Financial Officer, Chief Growth Officer, Chief HR Officer, VP of Sales, etc.

What are the qualifications to be a business consultant?

Business consulting is not a regulated field, which means that there is no governing body assessing a person's credentials to qualify as a business consultant. However, to be a successful business consultant that evokes constructive change, a successful business consultant must have a variety of qualifications that illustrate their worth to an organization. These qualifications are primarily broken into three buckets: formal education, hands-on experience, and other relevant experience.

Education

Most, but not all, consultants at the major consulting firms have an MBA, a masters in business administration. According to zippia.com, the breakdown of education held by business consultants is shown in the diagram below:

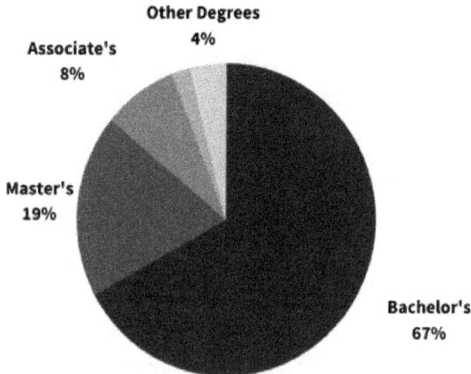

Source: www.zippia.com/business-consultant-jobs/education

Consultants who do not work for the major consultancies, typically have bachelor's degrees. However, most importantly, consultants should have the education needed for their area of expertise. For example, an HR consultant should have enough education, whether through higher education or certifications, to serve as an HR consultant.

Hands-on Experience

Many times, business consultants who advise organizations on a specific area of expertise, have had hands-on experience in that area of expertise. For example, software consultants, typically have experience advising and implementing software for organizations. Perhaps they were the software project manager for an employer previously. For most areas of consulting, consultants were employed in that field at one point or another.

Applicable Experience

Business consultants should hold relevant experience in the area in which they consult. For example, an IT consultant may have a lot of hands-on experience helping clients build their IT infrastructure, but if they have never applied that experience to banking clients, they don't necessarily have the applicable experience to work in banking.

Skills Necessary to be a Successful Business Consultant

Business consultants must have a variety of skills to support their work with businesses and organizations. The most important of these are considered the **The 5 Cs of Consulting**: curious, creative, communicative, credible, and collaborative. Additional skills include:

- Problem-solving
- Creative thinking

- People skills (active listening and observation skills)
- Great communication skills
- Change management expertise
- Organized with great time management skills
- Flexible
- Client-centric
- Demonstrates clear value
- Objective, concise, and clear
- Honest and trustworthy

Consider the doctor analogy again. Doctors who receive the best reviews and the most referrals hold the same skills as business consultants. They work diligently to resolve their patients' problems or ailments. When typical solutions don't work to remedy the problem, they are willing to think outside of the box. Their patients feel heard and well-evaluated, and they always leave a doctor's appointment with their questions answered. Additionally, patients' needs are always addressed in a timely, professional manner, and each patient feels like a priority to the doctor. A business consultant's clients should feel the same way.

Ultimately, a business consultant looks for the best ideas and practices, regardless of where they come from, to best solve problems and bring constructive change to the organization. Although organizations bring consultants in to solve problems and identify opportunities for growth and development, the best solution may arise from within the organization. Ego should be eliminated from the equation. As Peter Drucker stated, "my greatest strength as a consultant is to be ignorant and ask a few questions."

CHAPTER 2

Traits of Successful Business Consultants

"The single most important key to success is to be a good listener."

-Kelly Werstler

Kelly Werstler, a renowned designer, has delivered award-winning commercial, industrial, and residential design projects for global corporations, governments, and individuals. When asked what makes her different, she responded "The single most important key to success is to be a good listener."

As a Business consultant, the MOST important skill you must develop, hone, and practice is to be a good listener. While there are certainly other important aspects to this work, listening closely, compassionately, and analytically is THE most important facet of your work throughout the interactions with your clientele.

Consultants begin by understanding the issues from the client's perspective. Do not ever delude yourself into thinking you can walk in and immediately ascertain issues, pinch points, concerns, and solutions. Check your ego in these relationships as you begin to understand how the client sees their company, the work they do, from their unique perspective. At the start of every engagement, it is likely that the client will ramble, tell stories, and share their experiences; and while these may be somewhat disconnected to your work, this information will gain context over time as you learn more about the client and the nature of their company. These stories will hold nuggets of information for business consultants to retain and unpack; clients will share their stressors through these initial conversations, and your job is first to hear them. The stressors within an organization will emerge through these first conversations.

This is human nature! Have you ever had a close call in a car or on a bike or on a skateboard? If so, recall the color of your clothing, whether you had a jacket or coat on, the color of your shoes, or the temperature outside. What you most likely recall is the situation that created the panic: the impact point, pain, and/or triumph. Similarly, when clients are describing the situation that led to retaining your services, they will recall the issues that are affecting the quality-of-service delivery, systemic issues causing delays, the impact on revenue, or a decrease in the bottom line. While all of these are important, they are not the complete picture; that picture that will develop as you discuss more with various people within the business, and listen to the views and perspectives of all the participants.

Active listening skills will enable you to note the nuggets of information that the client discusses as a stream of consciousness. Subsequent conversations will provide context as the onion is peeled back to discover the underlying causes of the problems in the forefront of her mind.

In facilitated meetings, general meetings, and/or interviews, the value obtained from those interactions is not derived from what you say, it is derived from what you hear. And you cannot listen if you are talking!

In any engagement, you need to determine what success looks like from the client's perspective. That view can ONLY be obtained from listening to the client and is critical, not only to the engagement but also to your business. Client satisfaction only occurs when the delivery results in the satisfaction of success – in the eyes of the client.

During the time before the contract was signed, there were vague conversations about success, approach, and methods; your business was in "sales mode". Once the contract is signed, your delivery manager must now SET expectations for both sides so that there is a shared understanding of success. Specifically, when do we know we are done?

This is critical because projects tend to have "scope creep", which is an active, but not malevolent, push by clients to say, "well this is within the scope". Only with a documented scope can this sort of action be qualified as additional work or change order.

However, good listening skills are not all that you need; it is also critical to create opportunities for collaboration, discussions, and growth, which means that organization is key.

Exceptional organization and the ability to help

others organize their operations is key, especially if you are working in a multi-client environment. Maintaining an organized flow of communication and planning takes discipline and time but it pays off in efficiency and accountability. Organization is also one of the most visible aspects of a business consultancy, and is the most obvious when it is lacking.

Being organized means:

a. **Create and Follow Meeting Agendas:** agendas for all meetings are sent out at least 72 hours in advance to all attendees and then following the agenda. If you don't have an agenda, how can people prepare, know what is being discussed, and/or when the meeting is over?

b. **Assign a Designee to Take Meeting Minutes:** meeting minutes for all meetings, hopefully, taken by a designated member of the team whose sole purpose in attendance is to take notes of the meeting. Remember that we cannot take notes and speak or facilitate or present at the same time. Ideally, recording a meeting enables the verbal, and possibly audio, elements of the meeting to be recorded. The recording still needs to have meeting minutes done so that Q&A, resolutions, and action items can be documented, along with tasking specific team members for actions. Minutes out to the team or posted on the team/project wiki within 24 hours!

c. **Create and Maintain Accurate Records:** creating and maintaining a chronologic record of the artifacts of the project is critical, and this means all emails, documents, white papers, problem statements, solution options, evaluations, graphics, slide decks, etc. Think of this as the laboratory notebook of a researcher attempting to find a solution to a problem. This repository can be used during and after the project to improve processes, identify issues and look retroactively into decisions to understand their impact. Additionally, creating and keeping an "issues log" so the issues can be identified, assigned, tracked, and/or deferred to a subsequent phase of the project".

d. **Assign Tasks:** ensuring the project plan and schedule are communicated to all parties involved with actions assigned where appropriate. Understanding and publishing the critical path to success so that all can understand, contribute, and measure incremental progress to success. Project resources need to understand their tasks and the relationship/dependencies of their and others' tasks to the objective.

e. **Be punctual:** It is better to be an hour early than a second late. Timing is set for a purpose and shouldn't be interpreted in a lackadaisical manner. Train your staff to be on time or ahead of time and if a team member arrives late, restart the meeting! Yes, restart the meeting from the beginning. The peer pressure on the late team member will reinforce punctuality without you having to lift a finger. Team members are client staff also! No special treatment – punctuality will ensure that deliverables are on or ahead of time!

Oral and Written communications.

While pictures may be worth a thousand words, there will always be the need to communicate with other team members. The methods differ but both oral and written methods will exist during the life of the project. While there may be a tendency in some team members to be forceful and/or passionate in the conduct of a project, there is absolutely NO place for anything other than even-tempered conversations– EVER! Swearing, yelling, and talking over others must be controlled and stopped. All team members have value, or they wouldn't be on the team, all should be treated with respect and dignity. If a team member can't abide by respect and dignity, then they shouldn't be on the team – no matter their skills.

As a business consultant, you have a responsibility to your business, your client, and your co-workers to enforce respect and dignity in all your interactions.

With respect in mind, you also perform as Devil's Advocate. Specifically, you should challenge all solution options to ensure that all aspects of the problem have been addressed, not just the happy path! Too many times, in a desire, or rush, to be responsive, the options proposed aren't evaluated for all possible scenarios. This can be particularly embarrassing during a presentation when a customer challenges the recommendation with a very simple contrary scenario; one you didn't consider and don't have an answer for.

As a consultant, you cannot fall in love with a solution because you personally like it or professionally it leads to more work. You need to be an independent evaluator of every recommendation you make; the pros and cons are equally presented and addressed. Remember, every solution you present will be a compromise of some sort. There is an adage that there are 3 legs to every solution: cost, schedule, and quality. And, with two hands you can only pick two – so, the 3rd will always be a compromise. In your Devil's Advocate role, you should pick each of the 3 possible two-hand options so you can identify the pros and cons of each option. Pick the one that has the least compromise!

Discipline in this regard provides an additional layer of confidence to your team and, more importantly, your customer, that you have evaluated the options available and recommended the one you consider the best.

Applying this sort of discipline also mentors the team in how to provide quality products/services to your customers; you build the team that succeeds you and enables the business to expand. Do not fall into the ego trap of feeling irreplaceable. There is always someone better than we are and at the most inconvenient time, they surface. So, solicit ideas from everyone, no one has a lock on good ideas; be inclusive in your analysis of the problems at hand; and, prepare for the future by mentoring those on your team.

"It doesn't make sense to hire smart people and then tell them what to do. We hire smart people so they can tell us what to do."

– Steve Jobs

CHAPTER 3

Leveraging a **SWOT** Analysis

"What is good in the present is Satisfactory, good in the future is Opportunity, bad in the present is a Fault, and bad in the future is a Threat."
— Albert Humphrey (SWOT Analysis, n.d.)

Albert Humphrey developed the original SWOT analysis in the 1960s with colleagues at Stanford Research Institute. (Foresight University, n.d.) Originally, the developers used the acronym SOFT, which stood for strengths, opportunities, failures, and threats. SOFT quickly evolved into SWOT, which stands for strengths, weaknesses, opportunities, and threats.

Before SWOT analysis was developed, corporations struggled to create successful business plans, so Humphrey and his colleagues led a research project at Stanford

University to study data from top companies to understand why corporate planning was failing. Through their research, they discovered the key critical areas of a business that needed evaluation, including strengths, opportunities, faults, and threats, and that the areas of products, services, processes, customers, distribution, finance, and administration needed careful analysis. According to Mike Morrison in his article, "SWOT analysis (TOWS matrix) Made Simple", Urick and Orr changed faults to weaknesses at a conference in 1964, and SOFT became forever changed to SWOT. (Morrison, 2016)

Recently, businesses and consultants have advocated adding an additional T (SWOTT) to account for trends in the market, industry, or other societal factors that may impact individual businesses.

Since the emergence of the SWOT analysis, businesses and business consultants adopted this process as diagnostic tool to assess the current status of a business. Just like a physician uses basic diagnostics like checking weight, blood pressure, temperature, throat, lungs, and reflexes, consultants use SWOT as their primary diagnostic when determining the basic state of the organization. This is helpful in gaining a baseline understanding of the entity, and since consultants drive constructive change, and catalyze and implement effective change, consultants and their clients need to understand the organization's current vitals, strengths, weaknesses, opportunities, and threats. A SWOT analysis can help an organization with:

- Business planning
- Achieving goals
- Assessing risks and trends

- Decision making
- Identifying opportunities

A SWOT analysis is designed to create a realistic fact-based, data-driven evaluation of the strengths, weaknesses, opportunities, and threats facing the organization. The diagnostic tool takes emotion and perception away from the founders, business owners, and/or potential other leaders within the organization and draws the analysis back to fact versus opinion.

Understanding the SWOT+T Analysis

STRENGTHS

Strengths describe how an organization excels and what separates it from their competition. For example, employees, finances, location, cost advantages.

WEAKNESSES

Weaknesses describe factors that stop an organization from performing at its optimum level or puts it at a disadvantage. These are internal areas of need. For example, low employee morale, declining sales, the absence of new clients.

OPPORTUNITIES

Opportunities refer to external factors that could give an organization a competitive advantage. For example, new technology, new training, partnerships, change in policies and/or government, diverse market.

THREATS

Threats refer to external factors that have the potential to harm an organization and cause concern. For example, a rise in unemployment, interest rates, increased competition,.

+

TRENDS

Trends refer to factors in the industry, policy, society, government, etc., that can have a significant impact on an organization. For example, digitization, social media, the gig economy.

Strengths and weaknesses are internal to the organization, which means that these are things that organizations have control over and are often things that organizations can change. Opportunities, threats, and trends, however, are external to the organization, which means that organizations have little to no control over these things, and while individual organizations have little impact on these external factors, they can look to the future to address these issues ahead of time, rather than react to them.

The benefit of consultants in SWOT analysis

An experienced external facilitator or consultant works to ensure unbiased input and allow all leaders to fully take part in the SWOT analysis. An external facilitator will be unbiased and uninvolved in "office politics". A consultant will simply lead the group, not manage or dictate to the group because they do not have an agenda that they are selling. Consultants are seasoned at facilitating SWOT analysis, and they are good at listening, communicating, and facilitating group discussions.

Steps to follow when conducting a SWOT analysis

1. Define the Focus.

For a consultant to conduct a successful SWOT with a client, the focus of the SWOT should be clearly stated, first. For example, a SWOT's focus can be on the long-term vision for an organization, used to help identify the brand's strategy. However, a SWOT's focus can be on something more short-term like assessing a client's accounting software. Therefore, in the above examples, a consultant may want to introduce the SWOT with a clear statement such as, "We are conducting a SWOT analysis to understand the long-term vision of the organization's brand," or for the other scenario, "We are conducting a SWOT analysis to understand the impact of continuing to utilize our current accounting software."

2. Define the Roles and Responsibilities.

The consultant should serve as the facilitator, and the facilitator works with the team to help them decide what the rules of the process look like. Then, it is the job of the facilitator to make sure that everyone follows the rules. The facilitator is responsible for creating an atmosphere for everyone to feel comfortable and safe to engage in open dialogue. Everyone on the team is responsible for participating, and if "homework assignments" are given during the process, the members are held accountable to complete those "homework assignments" on time.

Who should serve on the SWOT analysis team?

For the big picture, long-term business strategies, the organization's founders and leaders must be deeply involved, which means if there is a Board of Directors or Executive Team, they must be actively involved in the SWOT analysis. However, for short-term business strategies, the founders and executive leadership may not need to be involved. For instance, in the accounting software SWOT analysis, the accounting team and a representative from each department within the organization may need to be involved.

3. Plan.

The consultant is the facilitator, which means everyone looks to the facilitator for direction. Make sure that each SWOT analysis has focus and direction. Each SWOT analysis meeting should have an agenda, and the agenda should include time for presentations of "homework assignments", as well as brainstorming time. The facilitator monitors the time and keeps the meetings on track.

4. Be prepared with open-ended questions.

The consultant drives the meeting and fosters open communication. To conduct a meaningful SWOT analysis, open-ended questions must be asked. The consultant should have a laundry list of open-ended questions for each area (strengths, weaknesses, opportunities, and threats), and then allow everyone on the team to answer the question. The consultant should never let a few people dominate the SWOT analysis. The key is to get everyone on the team to participate. At the end of this chapter, we list some open-ended questions that we use during a brand strategy SWOT analysis. These are questions that prove useful for a variety of SWOT analyses.

5. Assess and dive deeper.

Another reason why people hire consultants is that they ask hard questions. The consultant should be stepping back during the brainstorming phase of the SWOT analysis and listen and assess. When the brainstorming begins to slow down, this serves as an opportunity for the consultant to step in and ask some thought-provoking questions to help the team gain different perspectives or insight. For example, during a brainstorming session, you may hear the team discuss a lot about the internal employee perspective. This is the consultant's opportunity to ask the team, "What do you think your customers, prospects, and/or vendors think about that?"

Also, it is the consultant's responsibility to drive the conversation back to data. When people share opinions without any backup data, the consultant can ask questions like, "Wow. That is interesting. What report(s) demonstrates this trend you are discussing?" The consultant is tasked to ask hard questions and to help the team not fall victim to office politics or short-sightedness.

Conducting surveys with staff and clients/customers gives the organization and the consultant a more accurate view. Sometimes business owners and management are not always open to assessing negative aspects of an organization. To assess strengths, weaknesses, opportunities, threats, and trends research is required of employees, shareholders, target market, local industry, and national/international industry.

6. Report.

The consultant helps bring the SWOT analysis together by connecting the dots. For example, the consultant can ask, "How does the inability of integrating the accounting software into the CRM affect sales team retention and their common complaint of not being able to predict their commissions?" The consultant should help the team create a visual of the SWOT analysis so that the SWOT analysis can be reviewed continually. We recommend creating a SWOT template for you to use with your clients.

SWOT analysis with strong personalities

To ensure that everyone feels heard, we recommend that the facilitator of the SWOT meeting asks the participants a question. Then, each person writes their answer on a sticky note. The facilitator will have the question written down on an actual or virtual whiteboard/chalkboard, and each person will submit a sticky note to the facilitator for the facilitator to transpose as an answer to the question. There are no right or wrong answers. Then, the participants can look at all the answers and help the facilitator group similar ideas together. This activity may spark new insight!

Questions that a brand strategy SWOT facilitator/consultant should consider

STRENGTHS: Where does your organization excel?

- What does the organization do well?
- What does the organization do that its competition can't?
- Why do clients/customers come to the organization and/or stay with the organization?
- What are the organization's financial resources?
- Are the organization's revenue streams diversified?
- How is the organization's cash flow?
- Is the organization meeting its sales forecasts?
- What kind of assets does the organization have?
- What are the benefits of the organization's space and building?
- What kind of equipment does the organization own?
- What kind of intellectual property does the organization have? (trademarks, patents, etc.)
- What do you have in place to attract and retain top talent?

- Who are the key players?
- How's staff turnover?
- What professional development opportunities are offered?
- What processes make the organization efficient?
- How have you saved time or resources with a new tool or approach?
- How good is the organization with delegation?
- What kind of work culture does the organization have?
- Are the organization's values visible to customers and employees?
- How does the community view the organization?
- What is the LTV of customers/clients?
- What plans does the organization have to improve its market position?
- What are the growth plans?
- What's the main obstacle to growth?
- Are there certain sectors where the organization can grow but competitors cannot?

WEAKNESSES: What puts your organization at a disadvantage?

- In what areas does the organization struggle?
- Are there reasons customers/clients choose competitors?
- What stops the organization from performing its best?
- How do financial resources hold the organization back?
- Does the organization get its revenue from one mainstream? If so, is diversification a concern?
- How is the organization preparing for its financial future?
- Are any physical assets causing a problem?
- What condition is the office in?

- What condition is the organization's remote office setup?

- What condition is the organization's equipment in?

- Are any of the patents, trademarks, or copyrights in jeopardy?

- Is there any government red tape keeping a patent from moving forward?

- Does the organization take too long to file for patents, etc.?

- What kind of human resources do you have?

- Are there any departments that are lacking or inefficient?

- Are employee programs in place to improve the organization? If so, are they working?

- What areas could be improved upon when it comes to workflow?

- What slows you down?

- Where has the organization made mistakes?

- Describe the company culture that has been created.

- How does the public see the organization?

- What position in the marketplace does the organization hold?

- What are the organization's growth plans?

- How are competitors growing in ways that the organization is not?

- What is preventing the organization to grow?

OPPORTUNITIES: What are external opportunities for the organization?

- How does the economy look locally?

- Will the economy allow the target market to purchase more?

- Are economic shifts impacting the target audience?

- Is the price of materials going down?

- How is the market changing?

- Does the organization expect an increase in grants/fundraising? (Nonprofits)
- Any new contracts (assured new income)?
- New loans or investment funding?
- How will funding impact the organization?
- Does the organization expect a positive shift in political support?
- What opportunities could be created with new political allies?
- Are positive changes happening within any outside business relationships?
- Are vendors changing or expanding?
- Has a partner decided to move on, creating an opportunity to work with someone new?
- Any shift in regulations that could lead to positive change?
- How is the demographic shifting?
- Is the audience expanding, and, if so, how can the organization capitalize on this increase?
- Is there a new product or service that would allow the organization to gain new market share?

THREATS: What external factors could be a cause of concern for the organization?

- Is the economy in the organization's area in a recession?
- Will the economy negatively impact the customer's/client's ability to make purchases?
- Are economic shifts happening that impact the target market?
- Is there more competition in your market that's pushing the organization out?
- Does the organization expect to have changes in cash flow that would have a negative impact?
- Will funding changes hurt the organization?

- Is there an expectation of a decrease in grant funding or donations this year?

- Will there be a political shift in support? Should the organization be concerned?

- What regulation shifting could cost more money or hurt productions?

- What kind of negative impact could new regulations have?

- Are any outside business relationships changing?

- Is there any turmoil with partners or vendors?

- What threats accompany changing demographics?

- Is the target market changing in a way that the organization cannot accommodate?

Example SWOT Analysis

Situation: A financial advisory services firm, with one financial advisor, the owner, engages with you to understand why they have been unsuccessful in acquiring new clients in the last year. They want you to go straight to tactics to develop leads but to understand why they have been unable to acquire new clients, you recommend conducting a SWOT analysis with them.

Define the Focus: We are conducting a SWOT analysis to understand why the financial advisory firm has been unable to acquire new clients.

Define the Roles and Responsibilities: In this scenario, the roles and responsibilities appear quite clear. You will be the facilitator of the SWOT, and you will be asking the owner a series of open-ended questions. The owner's responsibility will be to answer the questions and all homework assignments throughout the SWOT analysis.

Plan: You create a schedule of meetings and deliverables over the course of a timeframe your client feels comfortable with. You hold the client accountable for attending the meetings and completing deliverables.

Ask Open-Ended Questions:

Strengths

- What do you do well?
- Tell me about how you acquired your existing clients?
- What do your clients believe you do well?
- What makes you different from your competitors?

Weaknesses

- Why do you believe you haven't acquired new clients in the last year?
- Tell me about the leads you received in the last year.
- Tell me about the meetings you had with leads in the past year.
- Why do you believe the leads that you met with chose to stick with their current financial advisor or chose someone other than you?

Opportunities

- How will the current economy present opportunities for you?
- How is the market changing?
- Tell me about current trends in your industry.
- Tell me about current regulations that are impacting your business.

Threats

- How with the current economy present challenges for you?
- Tell me about how technology is impacting your industry and where you stand with those changes.
- How does a weak stock market impact your cash flow as a financial advisor?
- What threats accompany changing demographics?

Assess and Dive Deeper: These questions provided an opportunity to ask deeper questions. Initially, the business thought the COVID pandemic played a major role in the inability to acquire new customers, however, when posed with the question, "What do your clients believe you do well?", there was no data to back up their answers. Therefore, you assigned some market research to assess client satisfaction. Additionally, you assigned competitive analysis homework, so more data could be analyzed and crossed compared with their financial advisory firm.

■■■■■■■■■■■■■■■■■■■■■■■■■■■

Report – After careful assessment, the SWOT uncovered the following:

- **Strengths**
  - Client retention
  - Trustworthiness
  - Strong response rate
- **Weaknesses**
  - Ineffectual sales process
  - Lack of value proposition
  - Client and audience confusion about the brand
- **Opportunities**
  - Growing younger generations that are not being targeted
  - Technology to conduct financial advisory meetings (COVID made this acceptable)
  - Offer packages that the large financial advisory firms don't offer but they can (with minimal cost)
- **Threats**
  - Online financial investing
  - Banks acquiring more market share by offering ease of use
  - Recession

The SWOT analysis served as an important diagnostic tool to be able to know what to focus on, what to change, and what to watch. The SWOT analysis drove action plans to help the client evolve and transform their business and processes to be able to acquire new clients.

How can SWOTs help business consultants grow their businesses?

- Helps consultants be focused on their approach while improving profitability and being more efficient.

- Offers a potential new service for consultancies, thereby expanding consulting engagements.

- Win new clients!

CHAPTER 4

Growing Businesses

"Growth is never by mere chance; it is the result of forces working together."

– James Cash Penney

James Cash Penney, the founder of JC Penney, knew that to grow a business, a team must be forged because success is not built by one but by many. In fact, he believed in sharing ownership, one of the founders of this practice, and he shared profits with those who made his success possible, including store managers. JC Penney was able to compete with Sears and Montgomery Ward because of following the Golden Rule, which was JC Penney's core belief. JC Penney relied on strong, ambitious, and ethical people to build the retail chain. James Cash Penney believed that they could make money and build a business by serving the community with fair dealing. Penney knew that to build a growing business you must have the right people and a clear purpose, and in Penney's case, that purpose was to serve the customer in the way the customer wanted to be served.

What is the main takeaway to learn from James Cash Penney? A business consultant must work with a team to help an organization grow. To grow an organization takes a team of strong, ambitious, and ethical people driven by purpose and to serve their customers/clients. The business consultant serves as one of many superheroes to drive an organization's growth.

What is growth?

Growth is a stage an organization reaches when it considers expansion or additional options to generate more revenue. Often growth is mistakenly defined as increasing sales only. While increasing sales is a component of growth, it is not the only driver of growth. For example, franchising, mergers, acquisitions, adding new target markets, and offering new products or services serve to grow organizations. Growth, which is scalable, is achieved by more than having a more aggressive sales plan or commission plan.

Tiffani Bova, Salesforce Global Customer Growth and Innovation Evangelist, said, "Many companies get trapped by the paradox of hitting numbers 'now' versus improving sales for future quarters or years ahead." Growth that is sustainable and scalable is not reactionary but methodical, based on long-term vision and strategic plays. As a business consultant, your clients will often call on you to help them grow their organization, and many of them will want to grow quickly or, perhaps, yesterday. (Insert chuckle here.) As Tiffani Bova stated, sustainable and scalable growth does not occur overnight. Growth is not a sprint but a marathon race.

What are the five stages of growth?

Launch Stage

Start-ups fall within the launch stages. At first, sales are slow, but they slowly increase. In this stage, growth is focused on acquiring new clients or customers through marketing and advertising their value proposition and competitive advantages. During this stage, costs are generally high, so many organizations may incur losses and not break even during this stage.

Growth Stage

During the growth stage, sales increase rapidly, and the organization finds that it has passed the break-even point and is now profitable. (This is a monumental occasion, which should be celebrated.) Profits don't typically increase as quickly as sales during this stage, but cash flow is positive.

Shake-Out Stage

During the shake-out stage, sales continue to rise, but not as quickly as in the growth stage. The reason for this is most often due to new entry of competitors in the market or approaching market saturation. Sales often peak in this stage, but profits may begin to decline.

Maturity Stage

During the maturity stage, sales start to drop slowly,

and profit margins may get narrower. Cash flow may get stagnant, as well. Capital spending is behind the business, so cash generation is greater than the profit on the company's income statement. This is the stage in which organizations will reinvent themselves in this stage by emerging in new or different markets. This is the stage in which an organization should reposition.

Renewal or Decline Stage

After a stage of success and profitability, an organization may start to decline in profits, revenue, external brand reputation, and internal structure. Indications of an organization's decline are when owners and leaders no longer show any interest in investing in technology or people but focus on a plan for their withdrawal. This is not all doom and gloom. An organization can renew its efforts before the decline stage sets in, but business leaders must be able to predict the change in the market and business beforehand.

How do the Five Stages of Growth Impact Business Consultants' Engagement?

As mentioned earlier, growth isn't simply about generating revenue and sales and building a successful and ambitious sales plan. Growth requires strategy and planning. Therefore, the business consultant must be able to evaluate which growth stage their client falls in. Knowing the stage of growth will help the consultant to understand the best way to advise and assist the client.

An Example: ABC Organization

Let's review this scenario with ABC Organization as an example. You have engaged with ABC Organization who has been in business for 10 years. Their revenue has plateaued, and they are losing many employees. ABC Organization has tried to grow the organization by partnering with other organizations, but the growth has not followed. The owner has indicated that they would like eventually to sell the business in ten years, and they would like to sell the business at top dollar. That is why they have engaged with you.

What stage of growth is ABC Organization in?

ABC Organization is in the Renewal or Decline Stage. They have maintained revenue and contribution margin, but its internal structure is fractured. The owner is not as passionate about the business as they once were, and now, the organization is simply an investment that the owner would like to capitalize on.

How does this impact the business consultant?

Now that the business consultant understands the growth stage of ABC Organization, the business consultant can better advise and serve the client. For example, the business consultant will need to think of a way to jumpstart growth again within the organization in such a way as to revisit the maturity stage. For the owner to get top dollar at the sale of their organization, they need to strategize in the following ways:

- Increase profit margins
- Grow the organization and show realistic growth projections for years to come

In this scenario, the business consultant, regardless of the subject matter expertise, needs to help stage the organization to be sold. Therefore, all advice and assistance the business consultant offers must be focused on the goals of the owner and future buyer(s).

What are some ways an organization can grow?

- **Joint Venture Alliance** – When two or more organizations form a separate business or legal entity to carry out business operations. An example of a joint venture alliance is Hulu. The Walt Disney Company, News Corporation, Comcast's NBC Universal, and Providence Equity Partners came together to create Hulu.

- **Partnerships** – Partnerships allow an organization to connect with existing organizations to grow. An example of a partnership is Starbucks and Barnes & Nobles. Starbucks' in-store coffee shops at Barnes & Nobles prove to be a win-win for both organizations. Barnes & Nobles and Starbucks were able to grow their brands by partnering with each other.

- **Licensing** – Licensing allows another company to use patents, trademarks, copyrights, designs, and other intellectual components in exchange for a fee or revenue.

An example of a license arrangement is Google's licensing agreement for Android.

- **Franchising** – By franchising an organization, you create a repeatable and teachable business operations system for you to sell to other entrepreneurs. A great example of this model is McDonald's.

- **Gaining Access to New Markets** – Gaining access to new markets means expanding into new markets. An example of successful expansion into new markets is Netflix. Netflix began in the US, but they have slowly expanded its service into other markets. In fact, Netflix is available for streaming in over 190 countries. (Help Center, n.d.)

- **Outside Financing** – When cash is limited, outside financing can be used to grow an organization. Examples include bank loans, angel investors, venture capitalists, etc.

- **Product or Service Expansion** – Product or service expansion means offering more products or services to gain more market share and drive growth. An example of this is Diet Coke. In 1982, Coke released Diet Coke to target and capture the calorie-conscious market.

- **Mergers and Acquisitions (M&A)** – Mergers occur when two different organizations join to form a new organization; whereas an acquisition takes place when one organization takes over another organization. An example of a merger is Exxon and Mobil, and an example of acquisition is when AT&T bought Time Warner Cable.

What are the advantages of growth?

When one thinks of growth they often think of attracting new customers or clients, scaling economies, establishing diverse revenue streams, increased brand equity. But these are not the only ways to create growth in an organization. As business consultants, it is critical to bring new perspective to clients so they can explore opportunities for growth they may not have considered. These advantages of growth lead to an increase in the top lines and bottom lines and provide a way to restructure the way that clients see their potential for growth.

What are the negative impacts of growth?

Growth can be a problem when it leads to shortages of resources, compromised quality in goods or services provided, the loss of control (or perceived loss of control), increased capital requirements, and/or increased employee turnover. To grow, businesses must be able to manage growth. Clients look to consultants for this guidance and to determine the best way forward. If a client is looking to grow the organization, it is up to their consultant to be a trusted advisor to counsel them on how to initiate scalable and sustainable growth. Simply growing an organization without having all the people, processes, and data to manage it can lead to the demise of an organization.

CHAPTER 5

Identifying, Supporting, and Changing Organizational Culture

"Culture eats strategy for breakfast."

-Peter Drucker

Peter Drucker, a legendary business analyst, writer, and influencer coined this phrase after studying different business, both successful and not.

What is culture and why is it important? You personally have a culture, we label it your morals, ethics, and philosophy. It is your guiding light in dealing with others, personally and professionally. As you grow your business, you imbue on that business your view on how to deal with others through interactions, policies on providing your services/products, and how you deal with problems, issues, and challenges. In the beginning, this "culture" will be observed by your associates and then replayed by them in dealing with customer situations. The culture will be handed around as tribal knowledge.

As you grow and provide written guidance for training, reinforcement and, to present to customers. The culture will then be codified in documents. It sets the tone for and of your business.

Here is a story of Jim (not his real name) whose painting company was contracted to paint a house while the owners were away on vacation. The house was really two houses, there was the main house which was approximately 7,000 square feet, and an attached in-law's house of about 2,000 square feet. Jim personally met with the owners, one of which was a friend since high school, to understand their desires for the painting job. Jim committed to the time frame and an approximate price for labor plus paint.

Two days later, Jim's design crew met with the owner to set the colors and paint types for each room along with an annotated picture of each of the colors/types of each room. The owner initialed off on each of the decisions and copies were made for both parties.

The job was completed on time but because of weather involved some weekend work for adequate drying time. It was the largest job that Jim's company had undertaken, and pictures were being taken constantly so brochures, the website, and flyers could be utilized for expansion of the business. In the process of the job, four new painters were brought on board.

The new painters compared this job to others they worked with other companies. They remarked that the paint used was premium paint, not a cheaper mid-range paint. They also said that with the prep work that Jim identified that the job would take longer than it should even though the results would "be about the same in the end". One of Jim's painters responded that "we were taught that the prep work holds the paint and that underlying flaws will project through the paint. A good foundation creates a good presentation and that is what Jim wants to achieve. We do it this way because it is the right way to do it, our way". The speaker unbeknownst to the new painters was Jim's middle son – just a painter in the company.

The new painters, to a person, commented that "other companies seek to make the most money using 'get by' methods and materials in the shortest time, even though the payment to us is the same." The back and forth with existing staff relayed that Jim taught us "the customer doesn't always see what we do, but we do. It is important that we paint their house as we would our own so the prep is what we would do, and the premium paint is what we would use on our own houses."

After the job was done, the new painters offered to introduce Jim's company to some housing developers with whom they had interacted. They also said that as the business expanded, they could recruit painters that shared the ideals of Jim's Business.

And, on return from vacation, the customer was completely satisfied and wrote a glowing thank you to Jim commenting on the attention to detail and their complete satisfaction with the paint job. About a month later, Jim got a call from two neighbors who had been to a party at the painted house, asking for meetings to discuss renovations.

A great story for sure and one that was the norm for Jim's company as it entered its sixth decade of operations.

The company is real, the second generation of painters is today preparing to hand the company to the emerging third generation. The company now operates in 7 states and is thriving.

Key takeaways that apply to every business

- The importance, methods, and emphasis the business places on the customer are not only words, but also actions; that is aggregated as the culture of the business.

- Staff will identify and then own the culture. They will share that culture proudly with other staff and customers. Every staff member that interacts with your customers IS the face of your business; make sure it is a good face.

- The culture will create opportunities for your business. Don't just look at the marketing opportunities – look at the referrals and references you build.

- The culture of the business transcends individuals, it will be carried and promulgated through the staff and customers. Look at the calls from neighbors after observing a customer's house.

As a consultant, you need to observe and listen to obtain a view of the culture of the company with which you are engaged. As you understand the view of success of your customer, you will analyze the people, processes, and data implications to move from point A to success.

Now, pay particular attention to the culture of the customer and whether the solutions you are considering are complementary to the culture. If so, then you have a reasonable chance of success. If, however, the solutions run counter to the culture, then you will have a rough time achieving success, if at all!

In the last decade particularly, there has been a

tremendous push to conduct business "digitally". While it is easy to say, doing it is an entirely different matter. And, most companies, large and small, have summarily failed at it. Want proof? Look at the companies that are heralded as having achieved the "digital" transformation and look at what they tout as accomplishments. Most, if not all, will say "we put the customer first" or "we put the customer at the center" of our solution. Every person reading this is a customer of some company, if not many, and as customers, don't you feel we should always be the focus? So, now turn that thought around and ask if your customers feel that way about the products/services they received from your business!

Jim clearly put the customer at the center of his business!

"Culture eats strategy for breakfast." Let's try to understand what Mr. Drucker was saying in these few words.

An Example: ACME Organization

Acme operates three manufacturing locations making products that are used by larger companies to create products for consumers. (Think about companies that make the wiring harnesses or electronic component assemblies for cars.) These component companies make items that are built into cars, so their customers are the car companies, not individuals.

Acme grew through acquisition, and two of the three locations were stand-alone companies prior to the acquisition by Acme; the most recent was 12 years ago. Up until the COVID 19 pandemic in 2020, Acme was profitable. But supply chain pressure, a drop in demand, and consolidation by some of its customers forced Acme to rethink its strategy for the future. The effects witnessed by Acme were an increase in time and cost of materials they needed to produce their products; a change in demand for products from each of their locations; and a regional change in their customer locations of finished goods.

Acme brought in a consultant to analyze options for the company to react to the new norms and present a strategy for the future.

Management viewed success as the company's ability to utilize its assets to address geographically disperse demand by its customers in a way that sustained quality at an efficient cost. They operated three production facilities, Plant A, Plant B and Plant C.

- **Plant A** was a five-day, 12-hour-per-day production facility that dealt with pulverizing rock into powder and then bagging the powder into drums for shipment. Quality checks were done by machines measuring the powder size. The workplace culture was to keep the inbound material sufficiently staged to sustain production during the day. This plant had been acquired.

- **Plant B** was a five-day, 18-hour-per-day production facility producing various aqueous solutions of different concentrations. Plant B utilized the product produced by Plant A for some of the products developed. The workplace culture was to provide the appropriate volumes of finished products with attention to the quality of each individual product lot run; all product lots started on Shift 1 to complete in a single day. This plant was owned by the company from the beginning of operations.

- **Plant C** was a 7/24 production facility product aqueous and solid products. Plant C utilized the product produced by Plant A for some of the products developed. The workplace culture was volume and quality standards for each lot of products produced, independent of which shift the lot started. This plant had been acquired.

The consultant worked with the company and its management to develop a plan using people, processes, and data as measures of work and success.

The phased change plan was to get all plants operating 7x24 in the first year with their existing product lines; no new products or lines would be introduced. Plant A would then transition to liquid product development in year 2. In year 3 all plants would be allocated product lines and volumes in coordination with each other and managed centrally. At the beginning of year 4, any of the plants could produce any of the company's products in the same elapsed time.

Production lines and associated processes were known to the company since they were in existence and operating at scale in plant C. The key to adoption and operation in plants A and B were primarily upskilling and augmenting the personnel (line and management) with skills to achieve the product variations and associated quality with shift-to-shift continuity transitions.

Clearly the company correctly observed that any change made to any of the plants would require the plant personnel to be aware of and support and endorse the change. It should be noted that plant A was unionized. The support of the union was solicited and asked to support the plan, which they did.

The analysis conducted by the consultant identified success as the harmonization of product production where, when, and in appropriate capacities to meet the changing demand of its customers. The regional production of products appropriate to the region to reduce transportation costs was addressed by all 3 plants products all products.

The ability to adjust to demand at each facility enabled demand on the company to be regionalized and adjust to demand spikes as a company, not as individual plants.

The production mechanics, chemistry, and product formulations were known to the company so other than normal R&D and improvements, no unknowns in the measurement of a new line were present. In addition, quality instrumentation, measurement, and standards were also known to the company.

Thus, processes and data were already known and just needed to scale. That left the people that needed to be capable of scaling and distributed demand apportionment.

■■■■■■■■■■■■■■■■■■■■■■■■

The key to success was in the people: staff and management at each plant and at the company. In addition to changes at each plant, a new department was created, copying from plant C, that would manage product development and allocation of product demand at a company level. Raising the staff skills and understanding of the required changes changed the culture of the Plants and thus the company to support the goals of the strategy.

Peter Drucker was spot on with his quote. Jim built the culture based on his personal morals and ethics. Acme changed the corporate culture based on a shared and adopted the vision of success. Both businesses reinforced the culture in words and actions and thus succeeded in moving from point A to success.

Jim's example illustrates how culture enables and supports the growth stage of a business. Acme illustrates how culture in a mature organization can be changed to enable a growth stage. Growth was the objective in both businesses, but the culture was addressed differently based on the maturity of the business.

Remember, if the hearts and minds of the staff, those that embody the culture of your customers' business are not aligned with, supportive of, and/or committed to the changes you are suggesting, success will be unachievable.

CHAPTER 6

Systems and Operations

"There's no great mystery to satisfying your customers. Build them a quality product and treat them with respect. It's that simple."

— Lee Iacocca

Operations in <u>any</u> business are geared towards managing your people to follow the processes to deliver quality products and/or services to customers. Do not be micro-focused to say, "well that means my delivery staff needs to be on point". While always true, the REST of your operation needs to be equally focused on the customer.

Let's look at what operations is in a business — everything except the CFO or CPA firm that must be independent to an extent from the business. Customer service, product development, information technology, accounts payable, accounts receivable, human resources, marketing, sales, etc. all comprise the operations of the business. You can argue the order but not the functions.

All these functions when operating in sync with each other makes for smooth, efficient, consistent, and repeatable operations. All the functions are geared towards providing the best customer experience in goods and/or services that your Business can deliver. If any of these functions is not operating efficiently then all the others suffer and, more importantly, it impacts your customers.

If HR isn't finding the right candidates and moving them through the interview cycle, then the function with the open requisition is operating below an optimal level. If customer service isn't efficiently handling a customer request, it is likely the customer is dissatisfied, and the root cause of the issue is probably still causing issues for others. And the list goes on.

Applying the SWOT analysis to the systems and operations, consultants can utilize the first two categories, strengths and weaknesses, to dig into the business operations at an internal level.

From an Operations perspective:

- Strengths will be areas of focus for competitors as they seek to address your strengths with lookalike or equivalent offerings.
- Weaknesses will be highlighted by competitors to minimize your strengths and highlight their strengths.

There are many individuals within an organization who can be assigned tasks that keep the company competitive. Consultants should be aware of these roles, and advocate for them to be filled by various individuals or departments within an organization. For example, who keeps an eye on competitors and how they stack against the organization? If companies do not know who and what their competition is and what they are offering, then how can they compete for customers or prospects?

Additionally, who in the company ensures that their staff is trained, current on processes and policies, and understands their offerings? Again, you pick the name of the group and/or person but if you have a new hire and provide no training then how do you know they have been exposed to ALL that your business offers?

Moreover, who communicates new offerings, support, or issues to customers and prospects? A combination of internal folks does but they need a forum to provide that information and obtain information and feedback.

This list is not exhaustive, but the point is clear that operations are the coordinated management of the various elements within the business that support existing customers and acquire new ones. This process does not need to be overly complex, and often it is best to keep it simple and easy to manage. Lastly, someone – a single person – needs to conduct the orchestra of the business; be held accountable to customers for good and bad; lead the charge to stay current in the marketplace; and have a passion for customer support.

Operations are measured on success in delivering customer satisfaction. Every piece of feedback from customers, prospects, competitors, and/or the marketplace is analyzed and changes to people, processes and the data measurements thereof are modified. A cycle of continuous improvement built into the culture will ensure the ego of the business and the staff are held in check and only confidence will emerge.

So as a consultant, look at how operations are measured and managed with your customers. The key to success may be nothing more than an improvement in operations.

Here is an example that hopefully sets this context.

Tony Hsieh identified a disruptive method to selling women's shoes in the early 2000s. At that time, the shopping paradigm was to go to a mall and pick out a style of shoe and try it on – if your size was in stock and the size run of that shoe matched your past buying experience. Sizes are general guidelines for shoes – there is no real standard for sizing a shoe. And there aren't width variations generally in women's shoes.

The frustration of finding the shoe in your size was the typical answer to the question "how was your buying experience?". So, Tony's selling proposition was "pick the shoes you like, order the size you think plus 1 up and 1 down. Try them on in your home and keep the ones you want and ship the rest back to us. We'll pay for shipping the shoes to you AND back to us. You, our customer, are the focus of our company, if you are happy, then you will recommend us to your friends and family".

Wait!!!!! I can order as many shoes as I like in a few different sizes and then I ONLY pay for the ones I keep, and I don't pay for shipping in either direction. What's the catch?

Yes and no catch was the answers!

The result was mind-boggling resulting in Amazon buying Zappos and adapting the model to apparel.

But the business model was transformed INSIDE Zappos to its day-to-day operations. Customer service reps were not only empowered to satisfy customer requests but encouraged to find deals on behalf of customers. And every person in Zappos, from Tony the CEO to the maintenance personnel in the warehouses and offices, was REQUIRED to personally write a thank you card to a REAL customer 2X a week and to identify themselves by first name and badge number. No typing notes, ALL notes were handwritten and addressed.

This reinforced the value of customers to the company throughout the company, all aspects of the company, and all functions of operations! As Lee Iacocca stated, "it's just that simple".

CHAPTER 7

Understanding Accounting and Budgets

"You have to understand accounting and you have to understand the nuances of accounting. It's the language of business."

– Warren Buffet

Regardless of your expertise as a business consultant, there is a common language shared among all business consultants and business founders, owners, and leaders, and that common language shared is accounting. The accounting language unifies the organization and provides financial information to its shareholders, and to be clear, the financial information shared provides clarity to the financial well-being of the organization, as well as the components of the organization. Unless you are an accountant, financial advisor, or CPA offering accounting and financial services, you need to understand key accounting terms, like revenue, direct costs, indirect costs, gross profit, and budget, and you need to be able to understand three key financial statements, the income statement, the balance sheet, and cash flow statement.

Before technology advancements, accounting served as the primary and sometimes only data source for organizations. Accounting notes the profits, losses, credits, and debts, and accounting's reporting is based on facts or numbers, not on opinions or words. Therefore, the information that accounting provides is rooted in historical results, and it provides the information needed to know how to help the organization, grow, make money, save money, grow profit, and manage a strong cash flow.

Many high-ranking people in business, from corporate executives to small business owners, don't understand the basics of accounting. However, as business consultants, we must understand the basics. While our clients may have been able to grow revenues and profits for their organizations without knowing accounting basics, business consultants don't have the option of not knowing. There is always an opportunity to grow, and a business consultant's responsibility is to help their clients grow.

What are the 6 key accounting terms that all business consultants should know?

1. Revenue
2. Direct Costs
3. Indirect Costs
4. Gross Profit
5. Gross Profit Margin
6. Budget

Revenue

Revenue is the amount of money an organization receives. For many organizations, revenue and sales are one and the same. However, revenue can come in the form of grants, as in the case with many nonprofits. Examples of revenue include sales, service revenues, fees earned, and interest revenue (earnings an organization receives from investments it makes or debt it owns).

Direct Costs

Direct costs are the expenses incurred from creating a product or service. Examples of direct costs include labor, software, equipment, and raw materials.

Indirect Costs

Indirect costs are the expenses incurred from operating the business. These are costs are not tied directly back to creating products or services. Examples of indirect costs include office supplies, utilities, office equipment, desktops, phones, etc. Administrative costs like marketing, HR and accounting are indirect costs.

Gross Profit

Gross profit is calculated by subtracting the cost of goods sold (COGS) from revenue.

Gross Profit Margin

Gross profit margin is calculated by subtracting the cost of goods sold (COGS) from revenue and then dividing that figure by revenue. This percentage will indicate how much gross profit is generated on a percentage basis after taking costs into account. Each industry has a gross profit margin average, so an organization can gauge its performance by comparing its gross profit margin with the industry standard.

Budget

A budget is an estimation of revenue and expenses over a specific period, often annually, quarterly, and monthly, and they are evaluated on a periodic basis. Budgets are often made for organizations, departments, and even people.

Regardless of the consulting service provided by a consultant to a client, all consultants should understand where and how the organization drives revenue; incurs direct and indirect costs; generates a gross profit; reaches a gross profit margin and operates within a specific budget. All activities and decisions an organization make either contribute to revenue or costs, including whatever service or solution the business consultant provides. Therefore, the business consultant must understand the organization's revenue, direct costs, indirect costs, gross profit, gross profit margin, and budget, so the business consultant can know how their services or solutions can impact the organization's revenue.

Three key financial statements

1. Income Statement
2. Balance Sheet
3. Cash Flow Statement

These key financial statements serve as diagnostic

tools for a business consultant to gauge the health of the client. Much like a physician who uses a scale, blood pressure cuff, thermometer, these financial statements serve a way to evaluate the organization's health.

Income Statement

For a specific period, the income statement shows three factors:
- What the organization earns
- What the organization spends
- The organization's profit

The income statement helps the organization, as well as those helping the organization (like business consultants), understand the company's financial health. The income statement shows the efficiencies of the organization, as well as the deficiencies.

Here is an example of an income statement.

ABC Company
Income Statement
For the year that ended (XXXX)

Revenue

Gross Sales	$ 500,000.00	
Less: Returns and Allowances	$ (10,000.00)	
Net Sales		$ 490,000.00

Cost of Goods Sold

Beginning Inventory	$ 25,000.00	
Purchases	$ 50,000.00	
Direct Labor	$ 50,000.00	
Indirect Expenses	$ 20,000.00	
Inventory	$ 20,000.00	
		$ 145,000.00
Less: Ending Inventory	$ 30,000.00	
Cost of Goods Sold		$ 115,000.00
Gross Profit (Loss)		$ 375,000.00
Gross Profit Margin		77%

Expenses

Rent	$ 50,000.00	
Amortization	$ 10,000.00	
Utilities	$ 11,000.00	
Wages and Direct Costs	$ 115,000.00	
Commissions	-	
Supplies	$ 20,000.00	
Marketing	$ 75,000.00	
Logistics	$ 2,500.00	
Repairs and Maintenance	$ 2,500.00	
Miscellaneous	$ 3,000.00	
Depreciation	-	
Interest	$ 12,000.00	
Total Expenses		$ 336,000.00
Net Operating Income		$ 39,000.00

Other Income

Sale of Assets- Gain (Loss)	$ 5,000.00	
Interest Income	$ 5,000.00	
Total Other Income		$ 10,000.00
Net Income		$ 49,000.00

Balance Sheet

A balance sheet outline's an organizations assets, liabilities, and shareholder equity at a specific point of time. In essence, a balance sheet outlines what a company owns and owes, as well as the amount invested by shareholders. The reason why it is called a balance sheet is that the organization's assets (cash, inventory, property, etc.) should equal the organization's liabilities (rent, wages, utilities, taxes, loans, etc.) plus shareholders' equity (retained earnings). The balance sheet will indicate whether a company has borrowed too much money; whether the assets it owns are liquid enough; and if the company has enough cash to meet current demands. For a business consultant, this is powerful information.

Here is an example of a balance sheet.

ABC Company
Balance Sheet
For the year that ended (XXXX)

ASSETS

Current Assets

Cash	$ 7,314	
Accounts Receivable	-	
Inventory	$ 5,560	
Prepaid Expenses	-	
Short term investments	-	
Total Current Assets		$ 12,874

Fixed (Long Term) Assets

Long Term Investments	$ 2,310	
Property, Plant, Equipment	$ 14,442	
(Less Accumulated Depreciation)	$ (2,200)	
Intangible Assets	-	
Total Fixed Assets		$ 14,552

Other Assets

Cost of Goods Sold	-	
Gross Profit (Loss)	-	
Total Other Assets		-

Total Assets $ 27.426

LIABILITIES AND OWNER'S EQUITY

Current Liabilities

Accounts Payable	$ 9,060	
Short Term Loans	-	
Income Taxes Payable	$ 3,349	
Accrued Salaries and Wages	-	
Unearned Revenue	-	
Current Portion of long-term debt	-	
Total Current Liabilities		$ 12,409

Long Term Liabilities

Long Term Debt	$ 3,450	
Deferred Income Tax	-	
Other	-	
Depreciation	-	
Total Long-Term Liabilities		$ 3,450

Owner's Equity

Owner's Investment	$ 6,000	
Retained Earnings	$ 5,567	
Other	-	
Total Owner's Equity		$ 11,567

Total Liabilities $ 27.426

Cash Flow Statement

Cash flow statements show the sources of cash, and they help an organization monitor incoming and outcoming cash. An organization strives to maintain a positive cash flow so that the organization won't have to borrow money to keep the organization going. For an organization to grow, the organization needs enough cash to pay back loans, buy commodities, or invest in profitable returns. Without positive cash flow, an organization will go bankrupt. As a business consultant, this information will help you understand your client's cash demands, as well as provide you insight as to how you can better their cash flow.

Here is an example of a cash flow statement. (Jiang, 2022)

ABC Company
Cash Flow Statement
For the year that ended (XXXX)

Cash Flow from Operations	
Net Earnings	$ 2,000,000
Additions to Cash	
Depreciations	$ 10,000
Decrease in Accounts Receivable	$ 15,000
Increase in Accounts Payable	$ 15,000
Increase in Taxes Payable	$ 2,000
Subtractions from Cash	
Increase in Inventory	$ (30,000)
Net Cash From Operations	$ 2,012,000
Cash Flow From Investing	
Equipment	$ (500,000)
Cash Flow From Financing	
Notes Payable	$ 10,000
Cash Flow for FY Ended XXXX	$ 1,522,000

These documents represent the language of business, and consultants need to understand what each shows as well as the terminology throughout. More importantly, by understanding these terms and reports a business consultant is better equipped to understand the financial health of the organization, thereby knowing what areas of the business are working and what areas of the business are opportunities for improvement.

CHAPTER 8

Navigating Technology

"You've got to start with the customer experience and work back toward the technology - not the other way around."

– Steve Jobs

"The first rule of any technology used in a business is that automation applied to an efficient operation will magnify the efficiency. The second is that automation applied to an inefficient operation will magnify the inefficiency."

– Bill Gates

So, what should a consultant know about technology?
- If the desired customer experience has not been analyzed
- If the outcome of the business has not been analyzed

- If the processes to achieve the customer experience have not been put into place
- If the KPIs to measure the customer experience have not been defined
- If the staff is not trained and skilled in executing the processes that deliver the desired customer experience

If each the five items above have not been done, do NOT think about technology. Reread the words of Steve Jobs and start at the top again.

If you get here, then you have people skilled in the processes that deliver the desired customer experience along with the KPIs to measure and improve the customer experience. At this point, Bill Gates predicts that technology will now magnify the efficient delivery of the customer experience.

While technology seems to be the exciting part of the equation, as these two distinguished gentlemen have said in words and both amply demonstrated by their actions, it is merely and simply a toolset to make good things happen faster.

If you haven't watched <u>The Founder,</u> you should. According to IMDb, <u>The Founder</u> is a 2016 American biographical drama film directed by John Lee Hancock and written by Robert Siegel, starring Michael Keaton as businessman Ray Kroc. The film portrays the story of Ray Kroc's creation of the McDonald's fast-food restaurant chain, which eventually involved forcing out the company's original founders so he could take control with conniving ruthlessness.

Watch starting at 13:15 when Ray Kroc meets the McDonald brothers, and they proudly give Ray a tour of their restaurant. Pay particular attention at 14:20 to the "assembly" of the burgers. And, then observe the measures of success that Dick McDonald uses; he exhibits a relentless pursuit of improvement in efficiency. They created a process to make the food available within 30 seconds of order.

How did they get there?

After the tour, there is dinner among the three of them and the brothers recount how they got to what Ray has just seen. At 20:00 the brothers outline the process they used to become efficient. They shut down a business that was making money – for months – so they could re-imagine it with the customer experience goal of 30 seconds from order to product. No technology at this point, the process first, then training and KPIs to measure performance – done on a tennis court with chalk lines.

After the tennis court mockup, they arrive at a scalable process to deliver 30 second cycle time. Having the process and skills required for their staff and the measures to ensure continued success, they NOW identify the technology they need to make this happen and build it! And they did this long before Bill Gates imparted his wisdom. The rest, as they say, is history.

THE takeaway from this story and the movie for a consultant is to identify a CLEAR picture of success. In the case of McDonalds, it was 30 seconds order to product in the customer's hands. In your engagements you need to first identify the picture of success. Without it you will not know if you have achieved it.

Then layout the processes, skills and measures that lead to success.

THEN layer on the technology. And, in today's world there a myriad of technology solutions. Not one of them is a silver bullet and all technology solutions fall short of perfect. However, heed Bill Gates' words, it is efficiency that we are striving for in delivering the customer experience.

Technology is ONLY a piece of that experience. Do not fall in love with the technology for if you do, it will typically lead to failure.

CHAPTER 9

Working Within an Ecosystem

"Innovation happens at the intersection of people, process, technology, customers, and business ecosystem."

– Pearl Zhu

Most people first hear the term ecosystem in their elementary school science class as a biological community of interacting organisms and their environment, and perhaps applied that concept to a pond ecosystem. For the living organisms within the pond to thrive, grow, and reproduce they are dependent on the living organisms and environment inside the pond, like the water, algae, protozoans, bacteria, plankton, fish, etc., as well as the living organisms and environment outside of the pond, like fungi, rotting logs, termite mounds, insects, birds, sunlight, heat, etc. The same is true for a business. A business relies on an ecosystem, as well, to thrive and grow.

According to Greg Sarafin, an EY Global Alliance and Ecosystem Leader, an ecosystem is

> "a purposeful business arrangement between two or more entities (the members) to create and share in collective value for a common set of customers. Every business ecosystem has participants, and at least one member acts as the orchestrator of the participants. All members in a business ecosystem, whether orchestrators or participants have their brands present in the value propositions." (Sarafin, 2021)

Let's break this business ecosystem down a bit. A business ecosystem must

1. be a business arrangement between two or more members,
2. create and share in collective value for a common set of customers,
3. have various types of participants
4. identify an orchestrator,
5. identify their brands in their value propositions.

Amazon exemplifies the business ecosystem definition. Amazon's members (suppliers, distributors, customers, and producers of complementary services) are in a purposeful business arrangement to serve consumers through online and physical stores while focusing on selection, price, and convenience for their customers. Members work together to create and share collective value for Amazon's customers. Amazon has a variety of participants within the ecosystem between the suppliers, distributors, customers, and producers of complementary services, and Amazon is the orchestrator of the ecosystem. Their brands are present in the value proposition so they can create more value for the members than if they were operating individually. Amazon offers web services, alexa, music, marketing services, payments, kindle, studios, video, fire, and business. Amazon has developed an ecosystem where a consumer purchases a product or service and is encouraged to use another product or service offered by Amazon.

Why should a business consultant work in an ecosystem?

Business consultants should want to work in an ecosystem for a number of reasons. First, consultants are subject matter experts, and bring specific and concrete expertise to enhance one or more areas of an organization. Consultants are typically specialists, and their expertise drill down to particular areas of focus. Therefore, bringing a variety of subject matter experts together to solve client pain points will address the pain point holistically.

Creating a network creates a higher value collectively than the members can create individually. Strategically, they can leverage various aspects of consulting to maximize their impact across a wide customer base, including time, capital, brand permission, market access, and other constraints. Additionally, members of a business ecosystem will inevitably collaborate on expansion efforts and will bring others within the network to support customers. Because of these, and many other advantages that come with an ecosystem, business consultant should within an ecosystem, where they create and share a collective value for a common set of clients. By working together in a business consultant ecosystem, business consultants provide additional value to their clients, and while they provide more value to their clients, the members of the ecosystem grow their businesses by ensuring the brands within the ecosystem are shared in their value propositions.

Big consulting firms like Deloitte, EY, KPMG, and PwC operate as ecosystems. They have subject matter experts and resources built internally and externally (third-party partner relationships) of their firm. Large corporations, governments, and nonprofit organizations hire these large consultancies because of the endless resources (ecosystem) that they can provide. However, small and mid-sized businesses and nonprofits cannot afford these consulting firms.

As a small or micro consultancy, you can provide increased value as the big consultancies do by being a member of a business consultant ecosystem. All the consultants or brands are promoted and known to each of the clients, and all brands must bring value to the clients. Therefore, the ecosystem proves to be a win-win situation for the consultants and the clients. The benefits of working in a business consulting ecosystem include:

1. Reducing the silo effect when operating as a subject matter expert. Digitization has forced interconnections between business units and service providers, requiring business units and service providers to work together to resolve pain points. The ecosystem provides subject matter experts from various business units and services to offer advice and guidance.

2. Working collaboratively and bringing in the necessary subject matter experts to solve client pain points, serving as a brain trust.

3. Practicing client centricity. Client centricity dictates a seamless customer experience, and an ecosystem can help provide that.

4. Accessing a wide variety of knowledge easily.

5. Strengthening customer loyalty by solving their pain points more systematically and holistically.

6. Developing new services and offering multidimensional solutions for specific customer needs.

7. Accessing new client groups.

8. Reacting more flexibly to customer pain points.

Let's review how a business consultancy ecosystem can work by reviewing the following scenario. This scenario is fictitious but is based on a real-life case study.

Jane Doe opened an amusement park a year ago, which was her life-long dream since she was a child. She invested and saved a great deal of capital to be able to buy the property and purchase and build the buildings, rides, and décor needed for the amusement park. However, she had no more money to spend, and she did not have a business plan. While she was driving revenue, she wasn't driving enough revenue to break even. She engaged with a marketing consultant to help her craft a business plan to get financing and to drive an effective marketing plan to drive more revenue.

What do you think the marketing consultant did? Do you think the marketing consultant issued a contract with Jane Doe for assistance with the business plan and marketing plan? The marketing consultant did not do that. The marketing consultant spoke with fellow business consultants who each held different subject matter expertise to see if they would be interested in working together to help Jane Doe. The business consultant ecosystem emerged with six business consultants. The marketing consultant served as the marketing expert and the orchestrator of the business consultant ecosystem. The client appreciated this holistic approach and signed the contract expeditiously.

From there the ecosystem grew to include vendors, media contacts, bankers, etc., and within a year Jane Doe's amusement park received financing and increased revenues. Could the marketing consultant have taken this on by herself? Yes. Could she have helped the client to accomplish their objectives? Yes, but by working within a business ecosystem, the objectives were reached in even a more effective and efficient way. The ecosystem was able to leave no rock unturned. The ecosystem worked together to achieve the client's goals. For example, when marketing made marketing campaign suggestions, the financial consultant raised financial considerations; the human resources consultant raised policy considerations; the technology consultant raised technological considerations; the engineering manager raised structural considerations; and so on.

Jane Doe attributes the success of the amusement park to the marketing consultant and those in the business consulting ecosystem still to this day.

Due to the limitations of not working in an ecosystem, small consultancies offer cookie-cutter approaches for small and mid-sized businesses and nonprofits in niche industries. For example, there are digital marketing agencies that target dental practices with a digital marketing solution that is the same for each dental practice client. By following

this model, costs are kept down for the consulting firm, and the consulting firm can offer its solution(s) at a very affordable price. The problem with this strategy is that the consultancy is not taking into consideration each entire dental practice, including its people, processes, and technology. Not all dental offices have the same strategies, people, processes, and technology. If that same digital marketing consulting firm served in a business consultant ecosystem, they would be able to provide more value to their clients by offering tailor-made solutions at an affordable price.
Small and mid-sized businesses and nonprofits want the following from their consultants:

- Tailor-made solutions.
- Evidence of expertise, knowledge, and experience.
- Hands-on approach.
- Frameworks to get pain points solved more quickly than without a consultant.
- Constructive criticism. (Clients want the status quo to be challenged, or they would not have hired a consultant!)
- Support and enthusiasm.
- Ability to educate and train employees, so that the client won't feel like they must be dependent on the consultant indefinitely.

Participating in a business consulting ecosystem affords you the ability to still own your own and/or manage your consultancy, but with the bonus of working within a team. Within a business consulting ecosystem, you no longer operate in a silo, and collaboration becomes the name of the game, for you and your clients. The business ecosystem provides a framework for you to run a client-centric business because the clients are the focus of the ecosystem. Finally, members of the business consulting ecosystem build strong relationships that will help each member grow and thrive.

Let's learn from the big consultancies. The big consultancies don't sell, necessarily, the specific consultants within their firms. The consultants come and go. The big consultancies sell because of how they link resources together to bring the most value to their clients. A successful small consultancy is a collaborative consultancy, and that can only be truly achieved through an ecosystem.

CHAPTER 10

Choosing Clients Wisely

"If people like you, they'll listen to you, but if they trust you, they'll do business with you."

— Zig Ziglar

One of the hardest lessons to apply to a growing consultancy is that even though a client may be interested in retaining your services, you also need to evaluate whether the relationship is beneficial to you. Not all paying customers should become clients. There are many reasons for this, and the most important is trust. Trust is a two-way street. Therefore, you must take steps to ensure that you trust the person and organization that wants to do business with you. Although it is difficult to turn away business, new and seasoned consultants must ensure that the relationship is cooperative, mutual, and reciprocal, and not all customers who want to spend money on a consultant are customers you want to have.

Remember that a part of your personal reputation is provided by your associates. So, too, is the case you're your business reputation. Your customers frame part of your business reputation. So, choose customers with an eye towards this when someone says," I want to hire you".

Clients will help you as much as you help them. Good clients will challenge and engage with you to drive the best results possible. This is the basis of MPWRSource, a place where people are empowered to achieve more.

Take the time to interview, yes interview, your potential clients. You are entering a relationship and you want to KNOW the person that will make this a 2-party relationship. There are four aspects to the interview.

Ensure that what the client expects of you is in your wheelhouse. If you are "in" to what they want and are competent in providing that, then both of you will benefit from this relationship. Your reputation will be enhanced with a satisfied customer and the customer will obtain the service desired. So, take the time to ensure that you can deliver what is expected.

Now make sure there is chemistry between you. This chemistry breaks down quite simply as able to engage and discuss at least the subject at hand. You aren't looking for a soul mate or life partner, but you are looking for someone with whom you can engage. Think of it this way. If you can't have a conversation about the topic that is bringing you together – the goal, objective, … of the business relationship, then how will you be able to deal with the challenges, decisions, and roadblocks that await you when you both commit to each other for this engagement? There must be some connection that you feel with the person across from you because there will be times during the subsequent engagement when you are sitting and discussing real topics of business that need honest and open conversations. Decisions that could enable or disable a business – either of yours!

During the conversations, you will determine whether there is a commitment to the engagement, and support from the top levels of the Business. If there isn't then maybe this isn't a job worth you committing to it – commitment should be joint by both parties. If you don't see it or feel it and hear it a few times prior to the start, then don't take a chance.

Finally, does the business have the financial wherewithal to engage with you? You are running a business and you should expect compensation. Unless you are doing this pro-bono! If the Business is struggling to raise funds, make payments, and stay current on bills, then part friends and wish them luck.

Keep this in mind, a contract engagement is a marriage for the life of the contract. All is good at the onset but then things happen, and the test of the relationship will be the ability to deal openly and honestly with the issues that arise.

The following five questions can help you gauge whether you should take on a new client.

Should I take on this Client?
5 Questions to Consider

1. Do I have the time to commit to this project?

Assess how many hours daily, weekly, and monthly this relationship will require. Based on your availability and current client base, is this something that you can realistically commit to for the duration of the contract? Do the expectations on your time meet your ability to serve this client and be present?

2. Do I have the expertise to advise effectively?

Assess the needs of the client. If they are asking for consultant to advise outside of your area of expertise, you many be tempted to take on the project, especially if it is an area in which you are hoping to grow. But the client's current needs require expertise now, not in the future. Do you currently have the expertise to support the client's needs? If not, do you have the ecosystem in place to bring in an advisor to support you?

3. Do I believe that disagreements between both parties can be solved amicably?

Disagreements and issues can and will arise. If this is the case with this client, do you believe that they will be able to navigate a discussion and options for a solution? This may be hard to gauge, but your negotiation process with any potential client can serve as a clue to this customer's approach to business. It is important to trust your instincts early in the relationship.

4. Do I believe that both parties are committed to success?

Working with a consultant can bring people outside of their comfort zone, and also requires commitment to learn, understand, adapt, assess, and evaluate from both sides of the relationship. Both the customer and the consultant must be committed to the success of the relationship and also to the success of the business the relationship is serving. Does the customer seem committed to the success of their business? Are they willing to make changes that may incur costs? Are they willing to reassess their current systems and operations? Are you willing to work within the system as it exists to bring about the change you are recommending?

5. Is the customer able to pay for your services?

Your need to make sure that your time is compensated and assess whether a customer will be able to pay for your services as they are rendered. If a customer does not continue to pay you according to your contract, are you willing to cease your services? It is easy to get invested in the growth and health of a company, but it is important to recognize that you are not a volunteer or unpaid support system to a business that cannot pay for services.

Use these five considerations to qualify a potential customer and then move forward when you are confident that all four answers are unequivocally affirmative.

"Begin with the end in mind", Dr. Stephen R. Covey stated in <u>Habits of Highly Effective People</u>. Interview your potential customers so that you get the desired outcome for both of you, a satisfied customer.

CHAPTER 11

Difficult Conversations

"Failing to prepare is preparing to fail."

– John Wooden.

Difficult conversations essentially are conversations that cause anxiety for one or both parties. Hopefully, your difficult conversations with your customers will be around a product or service not meeting expectations. However, situations can arise where the workplace, staff, vendors, etc. can be the topic of difficulty. Objectivity and compassion are key to producing as successful an outcome as possible.

First and foremost, you need to distill the passion and emotion from the subject. Typically, you should wait 24-48 hours before raising the issue with your customer. This gives you a chance to think about the topic somewhat dispassionately and the time to consider other perspectives of those involved to ensure that the issue is real and not just you personally.

These conversations will generally fall into two categories: project/product related, and not. The "not" covers everything that isn't project/product related and that covers innumerable dimensions which we will refer to as "personal". Not meaning you personally but a person that is encountering challenges; and you believe that the topic needs to be raised with your customer.

The project/product-related conversations, which will be the most frequent, will typically involve some sort of missed expectation. Quality, timeline, completeness, etc. of a project/product. Before having the conversation ensure that you have all the factual aspects covered and understood. Then think about the customer's concern from their viewpoint. Is this personally affecting them in some way? Presentation to a supervisor, element of a promotion, cost impact, budget break, performance KPI, etc. The more you can understand why this is an issue, the better equipped you will be to curate the conversation.

The conversation should be just that, a conversation. Do not come equipped with a slide deck, document, etc. Those artifacts will immediately set the tone of the discussion (no longer a conversation) to be antagonistic. You sit with the customer and ASK the customer to level your understanding of the issue from their perspective; this sets the tone to be one of respect and consideration. Now listen and do not interrupt.

When the customer is finished, pause for a moment. If this is half an hour or more, stand up to stretch your legs

or ask for a bio break or coffee or water. Reflect on what you
heard. Did you hear what you had prepped for? If so, then
come back and respectfully begin the dialog by highlighting
key things, of all the things the customer said, that need to be
addressed. Boil the key things to a handful (5 or less) and
then get an agreement from the customer that these are the
key things needed to resolve the issue. When you get an
agreement ask for a follow-up meeting in a day or two and
then thank the customer for the opportunity to discuss the
issue. Suggest that you have some regular dialog, in or out of
the office, to ensure "unofficially" that things are on track for
both sides. Then cordially leave and resolve the handful of
key things so the meeting in a day or two shows you care
enough about the relationship to work them.

If you didn't hear what you prepped for, then you
need to come back from the break and get ALL the
information you need from the customer to address whatever
is going on. Start by saying something to the effect "well, that
was not at all why I thought I was meeting with you."
Honesty is the best policy!

When you begin again, recite what you heard so that
you have corroboration on the salient points of the issue.
Consciously explain that you need to take notes and you
would appreciate the customer's input to ensure the notes are
accurate; collaboration reinforced again. Customers will
appreciate this since it directly implies you are listening and
want to satisfy their concerns. When you two are finished,
thanks are again extended for the forthright nature of the
conversation; apologies for missing the point of the
conversation; and, depending on the time of day, let me
reconnect this afternoon/tomorrow on my next step with
you. Thank you again and goodbye!

Two things just occurred during these conversations. You extended your relationship with the customer on a professional and personal basis. You came across as non-confrontational with empathy for the customer's point of view. And you obtained that POV before asserting yours. You didn't come in guns blazing assuming you knew what the issue was and didn't present a defense to the prosecution. You were calm, open, engaging, and sensitive to the merits of the customer's perspective.

There are two outcomes of the initial conversation where you solicited the customer's perspective. In the former, you had done the research and could distill the issue into a handful of key items to resolve. But you allowed the customer time to express a point of view and you most likely learned something as well. In the latter case, you were completely caught off guard. Again, you learned something.

In both cases, you did not embarrass yourself or your company. You came across with empathy and compassion and respect. This underscores the need to constantly listen and react.

This individual will most likely work for another company at some point or advance to an executive level within the existing company. In either situation, your behavior will have left an indelible mark of reasonableness, and a true collaborator. This and other respectful conversations will weigh positively on you personally and your company professionally.

Now the "not" category of conversation. These can occur on either side of the equation it is not always you going to the customer, you may be called into a conversation by the customer.

"Not" conversations are workplace, personnel,

and/or personal behavior-related conversations. These conversations may represent an irritant issue or something as serious as a legal issue.

Some examples will set the context:

1. After work one day, the project team celebrates a milestone accomplishment. During the celebration, a member of your staff feels there was inappropriate action(s) by one of the customer staff members and reports to you that they now feel they want off the project or worse.

2. During a stressful meeting at the customer's site on the project, one of your team reports that inappropriate and disparaging comments were made which they consider borderline racial.

3. A team member reports to you that a certain member of the customer's staff is making suggestive comments and it is creating a very uncomfortable/toxic workplace.

The list of examples can continue but these are clearly not related to the project/product other than by the association of team members. Recognize also that these conversations can be on the customer side, and you just haven't gotten the invite to the meeting yet.

Follow the policies of your business regarding these sorts of reports. And again, treat these as conversations; empathy, compassion, and respect are key. The request for the meeting with you has already induced stress and anxiety;

do not add additional stress and anxiety. Thank the individual(s) for bringing this to your attention. Following your policies, gather the facts but, by any means possible, do not make the individual(s) feel like victims!!! No judgment, just support and encouragement noting that this is important not only for them but for you, your business, and the customer's business.

If on your side, put yourself in the customer's shoes – this will most likely be a shock to them. So, the conversation, while serious in nature, needs to remain a conversation. There is no accusation or presumed guilt or innocence. The issue reported needs to be handled jointly by you and the customer. And, hopefully, the opposite is true should you be the one that is shocked.

Totally dependent on the severity of the issue, some matters can/will be removed from your hands. However, to the extent that you can manage the conversation, keep it a conversation seeking a joint resolution.

The "not" conversations fortunately are not a common occurrence but that doesn't mean you don't prepare for them.

Difficult conversations will undoubtedly occur during any relationship with a customer. The key to not having them ruin the relationships is respect for both sides. And the first step in showing respect is to have a conversation where you listen!

CHAPTER 12

Building a Successful Business Consultancy

"Successful people are always looking for opportunities to help others. Unsuccessful people are always asking, 'What's in it for me?'"

— Brian Tracy

Brian Tracy's quote applies to all professions, and arguably to humans in general. However, for business consultants, this quote sums up the purpose of the profession quite well. Business consultants seek to help organizations grow. Business consultants exist to serve, and their priority is their clients. By adopting this core belief, a business consultant travels on the pathway to success because they know that by helping their clients succeed, they, too, will succeed.

Business consultants, including those whose focus is strategy, management, sales, marketing, accounting, technology, human resources, law, communications, risk mitigation, etc., provide advice, guidance, and/or deliverables to individuals and businesses in their area of expertise on a temporary or contract basis. In many ways, a business consultant is much like a mental health counselor. A mental health counselor provides support to those who are experiencing mental or emotional distress, and they provide a variety of techniques to help their patients. However, the most important skills for a mental health counselor include listening and asking the right questions. This is true for business consultants, as well, except for their focus is on business matters rather than mental health.

Throughout this book, we have discussed the foundations of business consulting. Each chapter highlights essential concepts and skills that all business consultants should obtain. However, to run a successful small consultancy, the business consultancy should follow the following six steps.

6 Steps to Run a Successful Small Consultancy

1. Assess your consultancy's strengths and skills.

Know your wheelhouse! If your consultancy is trying to determine its true strengths and skills answer the following questions:

- Where have I/we been successful?
- What do I/we enjoy?
- Do I/we have a unique point of view?

- Do I/we have the education and experience necessary to be an authority in this field?
- Is there a demand for your strengths and skills? If so, who demands these strengths and skills?

2. Create a business plan and brand strategy.

Most business consultants advocate for their clients to compose a business plan and brand strategy; therefore, business consultants should follow their own advice. According to GO Business Plans, "Those who finished their business plans were twice as likely to succeed in growing their business than those who have no business plans." (Business Plan Facts and Statistics to Drive Your 2020 Business Strategy) A brand strategy is required for all businesses, as well, because clients don't just buy products and/or services, they buy from those who have shared values. A brand is the way a product, service, organization, or individual is perceived by those who experience it. Therefore, it is up to the consultancy to ensure that each touchpoint a prospect or client has with your brand reflects your brand's purpose.

3. Invest in tools of the trade and continuing education.

Invest in tools of the trade. Practice what you preach to your clients. Invest in the necessary software, websites, business cards, etc. to run your consultancy successfully. Also, don't stop learning. A successful business consultant has a relentless thirst for knowledge, so the consultancy should continually invest in ongoing education and experiences.

4. Market the consultancy and build a repeatable system for attracting and closing clients.

Utilize digital marketing, referrals, networking, and a business consulting ecosystem to market the consultancy. Remember a diversified market channel approach is always the best approach.

5. Know when to say "no".

This is one of the most difficult lessons consultants learn. Every consultant has a story to tell about the time they should have said, "no". Knowing when to say "no" can save your consultancy. You should say "no" to a prospect or client when:

- The project does not fall within your offerings or skillset.
- You have the skillset but not the resources.
- The client is not willing to pay what you are worth.
- Core values are not aligned.

6. Participate in an ecosystem.

You have the benefits of owning or managing your business, but, as part of a business ecosystem, you are now part of a team. In the ecosystem, you can collaborate with other subject matter experts and not have to operate in a silo for you and your clients. The ecosystem fosters client centricity by focusing on client pain points, and you build long-standing relationships that will help you and your consultancy grow.

***

The information outlined in this book, will help you build a strong foundation for a successful consultancy. A reminder from Denis Waitley, an American motivational speaker, writer, and consultant is especially helpful in these circumstances. He says, "[D]on't dwell on what went wrong. Instead, focus on what to do next. Spend your energies on moving forward toward finding the answer."

ABOUT THE AUTHORS

Tiffany Joy Greene, M.BA. is an entrepreneur; educator; author; motivator; and strategy, management, branding, communications, marketing, and public relations consultant to SMBs, start-ups, consultancies, and non-profits. As founder of MPWRSource and its program, MPWRForum, she is on a mission to empower small businesses and nonprofits to thrive and soar; thereby strengthening communities. Additionally, as an advocate for often marginalized people, Tiffany promotes diversity, equity, and inclusion in her community. Currently, Tiffany resides in Chesterfield, Virginia, with her husband, Tim Quintavalle, and their two children and Yorkie.

Joe Romello is a mathematician/computer scientist by education, a serial entrepreneur in practice and a former Managing Consultant at two of the largest consulting companies in the US. A business transformation executive, he spends time supporting non-profit and for-profit companies adapting to their ever-changing environments. A firm believer that teams are what wins in business, he looks to coach and mentor people to up and cross-skill, as well as companies to have a balance of people, process, data, and technology to grow and thrive. Joe resides in the suburbs west of Philadelphia, PA, with his wife Amy and their two golden doodles.

www.ingramcontent.com/pod-product-compliance
Lightning Source LLC
Chambersburg PA
CBHW060632210326
41520CB00010B/1567